....

This book belongs to

....

Folded by

COLOR EDITIONS NO. 5

THE MEANING OF FLOWERS

LORE, LEGENDS, AND TALES OF OUR FAVORITE BLOOMS

STEPHANIE SCHWARTZ

Studio Fun Books
White Plains, New York • Montréal, Québec • Bath, United Kingdom

ArtFolds ™
Color Editions No. 5
FLOWER

ArtFolds is a patent-pending process.

ArtFolds and Studio Fun Books are trademarks of Studio Fun International,
Inc., a subsidiary of The Reader's Digest Association, Inc.

ISBN 978-0-7944-3332-1

To learn more about ArtFolds, visit artfolds.com.

Customized and/or prefolded ArtFolds are available. To explore options
and pricing, email specialorder@artfolds.com.

To discover the wide range of products available from Studio Fun
International, visit studiofun.com.

Address any comments about ArtFolds to:
Publisher
Studio Fun Books
44 South Broadway, 7th floor
White Plains, NY 10601

Or send an email to publisher@artfolds.com.

Printed in China   Conforms to ASTM F963

1 3 5 7 9 10 8 6 4 2   LPP/10/14

About ArtFolds

THE BOOK YOU HOLD in your hands is more than just a book. It's an ArtFolds™! Inside are simple instructions that will show you how to fold the pages to transform this book into a beautiful flower-shaped sculpture. No special skill is required; all you'll do is carefully fold the corners of marked book pages, based on the folding lines provided. When complete, you'll have created a long-lasting work of art. It's fun and easy, and can be completed in just one evening!

To add to the experience, each ArtFolds contains compelling reading content. In this edition, you'll read about the fascinating ways we have used flowers over the centuries, bringing beauty and meaning to our lives.

Each ArtFolds edition is designed by an established, professional book sculptor whose works are routinely displayed and sold in art galleries, museum shops, and online crafts and art stores. ArtFolds celebrates this community of artists and encourages you to support this expanding art form by seeking out their work and sharing their unique designs and creations with others.

To learn more about ArtFolds, go to www.artfolds.com. There you'll find details of all ArtFolds™ editions, instructional videos, and much more.

Instructions

Creating your ArtFolds Color Editions book sculpture is easy! Just follow these simple instructions and guidelines:

1. **Always fold right-hand pages.**

2. **Always fold toward you.**

3. All folding pages require two folds: the top corner will fold down, and the bottom corner will fold up.

1, 2

4. Grasp the top right corner of the page, and fold until the side of the page aligns exactly with the TOP of the horizontal color bar.

4

5. Grasp the bottom right corner of the page, and fold upward until the side of the page aligns exactly with the BOTTOM of the horizontal color bar.

5

6. Carefully run your finger across the folds to make sure they are straight, crisp, and accurate.

7. Continue on to the next page and repeat until your ArtFolds book sculpture is complete!

Extra advice

- We recommend washing and then thoroughly drying your hands prior to folding.

- Some folders prefer using a tool to help make fold lines straight and sharp. Bone folders, metal rulers, popsicle sticks, or any other firm, straight tool will work.

- Some folders prefer to rotate their book sideways to make folding easier.

- Remember: The more accurate you are with each fold, the more accurate your completed book sculpture will be!

Folding begins in just four pages!

For more folding instructions and videos, go to www.artfolds.com

THE
MEANING OF FLOWERS

LORE, LEGENDS, AND TALES OF OUR FAVORITE BLOOMS

SINCE ANCIENT TIMES, flowers have been appreciated for more than just their beauty. They are central players in countless myths and legends. They are used as medicines. And they are a universal way to express our feelings—especially those hardest to put into words. Flowers console us at funerals and celebrate with us at weddings; we present flowers as gifts to those we love and as prizes to victors, whether a contest of beauty or might.

The language of flowers reached its height in Victorian times, when special bouquets were assembled to communicate secret messages from one lover to another. Carefully selected blooms were a shorthand way to express affection and even to arrange clandestine meetings. But flowers have played similar roles in virtually all cultures over the millennia.

In *The Meaning of Flowers*, we explore the stories behind 40 of our favorite blooms. Here are their symbolic meanings; brief histories; the story behind their names; and intriguing facts and legends. They say a rose is just a rose, but when you also know the lore and history of such a beautiful flower, a rose—or daisy, or bluebell—becomes so much more.

AMARYLLIS

MEANING: PRIDE, DETERMINATION

A cluster of dramatic, funnel-shaped flowers bloom at the end of a tall, upright stem.

Because a flowering amaryllis is
so tall and bold, it came to symbolize pride
in Victorian England.

The amaryllis owes its name to
an ancient Greek tale of unrequited love.
The nymph Amaryllis fell hopelessly
in love with the shepherd Alteo,
who didn't give her a second look...

...The nymph decided to win his love by giving
Alteo the thing he desired most—a unique flower.
As she pierced her heart with a golden arrow,
the drops of blood that fell
onto the ground sprouted the striking
crimson flower today known as amaryllis.

ANEMONE

MEANING: FORSAKEN; UNFADING LOVE

Delicate flowers of many colors nod
atop thin stems.

Anemones are native to the Mediterranean.

In ancient Rome, anemones were used to treat headaches and stomach problems.

Anemones are associated with a
powerful Greek myth. When the beautiful Adonis,
beloved of Aphrodite, the goddess of love,
died after being stabbed by a wild boar, the white
flowers around his body—anemones all—turned
red from his blood before the petals dried up
and blew away in the wind.

ASTER
MEANING: LOVE, DAINTINESS

Delightful blooms feature sunny yellow centers surrounded by petals in rainbow colors.

Named for the Greek word for star,
asters were said to have sprung up wherever
stardust was scattered.
Their early English name is starwort.

If you're cutting asters for a bouquet, it's best to do so early in the morning—they'll last longer.

BEGONIA

MEANING: BEWARE

Long-lasting pink, white, red, or sometimes yellow flowers rise above rich foliage.

Begonias are eaten, raw and cooked, in many countries. The flowers have a slightly citrusy taste, and the leaves are delicious in salads.

There are more than 1,500 species and hybrids of begonias. Some varieties are only two inches tall, while others grow to six feet.

In China, begonias are used in remedies to clean wounds and to clear up colds and stomachaches.

Begonias will happily root in a glass of water.

BLUEBELL
MEANING: HUMILITY
Bright blue, bell-like flowers hang
suspended over delicate leaves.

Bluebells thrive in wooded areas, carpeting the ground with blooms in the springtime.

The scientific name for bluebells used to be
Endymion (today it is Hyacinthoides).
In Greek mythology, the moon goddess Selene
fell hopelessly in love with a young shepherd,
Endymion. Unable to have him for herself,
she cast a spell that kept him asleep forever so
she could continue to enjoy his beauty from afar.

Some believe that it's bad luck to pick bluebells because the fairies of the forest cast protective spells on the flowers to save them.

CAMELLIA

MEANING:

PINK: LONGING FOR YOU
RED: YOU'RE A FLAME IN MY HEART.
WHITE: YOU'RE ADORABLE.

Shiny, dark green leaves frame brilliant blooms
in red, pink, or white.

Although the flowers are strikingly beautiful,
camellias have no scent.

In Japan, camellias symbolize friendship and harmony. They were traditionally planted by the graves of Samurai warriors.

To grow beautiful camellias, water them
occasionally with a cup of tea.

CARNATION

MEANING: FASCINATION
PINK: I'LL NEVER FORGET YOU.
RED: ADMIRATION
PURPLE: CHANGE
WHITE: INNOCENCE
YELLOW: DISAPPOINTMENT, REJECTION

Frilly petals in all colors but blue rise
on narrow stems.

In the 13th century the Crusaders used
a mixture of carnations and wine to control
the fevers of the plague.

In the U.S., carnations were distributed
during the first ever celebration of Mother's Day,
and since then they have been an emblem
of that holiday.

Carnation petals are sweet and can be used in desserts, but the white bases are bitter and have to be cut away.

CHRYSANTHEMUM

MEANING: CHEERFULNESS
RED: I LOVE YOU.
WHITE: TRUTH
YELLOW: REJECTION

Decorative flowers, in colors from the traditional yellow to purple and even green, bring cheer in the cooler months.

The name chrysanthemum comes from
the Greek words for "golden" and "flower."
In feng shui tradition, chrysanthemums are believed
to bring happiness into your home. The petals,
used in salads, are believed to promote longevity.

A tea made from chrysanthemum flowers
can be used to help recover from the flu.

CONEFLOWER

MEANING: STRENGTH, HEALING

Lavender petals surround an orange-brown center; the coneflower's innocent appearance belies its health-giving powers.

Also known as Echinacea, coneflowers were used as healing herbs by many Native Americans. Tinctures were applied to wounds, burns, and bites; infusions were taken for headaches, stomachaches, and colds. The roots and flowers were made into a paste to clear up skin infections, and the roots were chewed as a thirst quencher and to reduce the pain of toothaches.

Some believe that if you carry a
coneflower with you, you will be strong
in the face of troubles.

Coneflowers are great in the garden—
the attractive plant has a long flowering period
and is self-seeding.

CROCUS

MEANING: CHEERFULNESS; YOUTHFUL GLADNESS

Bright little cup-shaped flowers appear in the
spring or autumn to hint at season's change.

Cleopatra, the famed beauty, used scented oil
of crocus to care for her hands.

One variety of crocus, Crocus sativus, is the source of saffron, a spice so expensive that it is sometimes known as "red gold." This crocus variety is one that blooms in the autumn.

Although it takes hundreds of crocuses to produce the saffron sold in spice shops, you can produce enough for home use with just a few plants.

DAFFODIL

MEANING: YOU'RE THE ONLY ONE FOR ME; REGARD

Petals surround a trumpet-shaped center, the flowers rising on tall stems to welcome the spring.

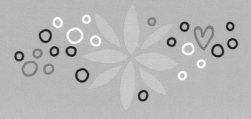

Never give someone a single daffodil—
there's a superstition that says a single flower
brings bad luck.

The daffodil is the national flower of Wales.

Daffodils are one of the flowers
mentioned in William Shakespeare's plays.

"When daffodils begin to peer,
With heigh, the doxy over the dale,
Why, then comes in the sweet o' the year..."

—THE WINTER'S TALE, ACT IV, SCENE III

There is a Chinese legend that says that forcing
a daffodil into bloom in your home over the
New Year will bring you good luck.

DAISY

MEANING: LOYALTY, HOPE, INNOCENCE, YOUTH

Commonly seen with white petals surrounding a yellow center, daisies can surprise with their array of color combinations.

While the daisy usually symbolizes innocence, in Norse mythology it's a symbol of love, fertility, and motherhood, associated with the goddess Freya.

Daisy extracts are used in skin care
and in remedies for bronchitis.

In medieval England, knights would include a daisy in their coats of arms to show that their love was not unrequited.

DANDELION
MEANING: HAPPINESS

Bright yellow flowers nestle among
jagged leaves—a gardener's nightmare but
an epicure's delight.

While many people consider
the dandelion to be a pesky weed, others enjoy it
as a highly nutritious spring vegetable.
Its leaves can be eaten raw in salads or cooked
to make them more tender and less bitter.
They're rich in vitamins A and C, as well as iron,
calcium, and potassium.

Dandelion roots can be ground and roasted to make a caffeine-free coffee substitute.

Dandelions are actually good for your lawn.
Their roots loosen and aerate the soil and pull
nutrients closer to the surface.

FORGET-ME-NOT
MEANING: MEMORIES OF TRUE LOVE

Clusters of tiny flowers in blue, pink, or white
bloom in the spring or early summer.

The forget-me-not is one of the few
true-blue flowers.

Forget-me-nots have the equivalent name in many languages, including Italian, German, French, Russian, and Danish. The name has been around since the 15th century.

Legend has it that a knight in full armor was walking along a riverbank with his ladylove. As he bent to pick some blue flowers for her, he fell into the river. Drowning, he tossed the flowers to her, crying, "Forget me not!"

FORSYTHIA
MEANING: ANTICIPATION

Vivid yellow flowers covering the long branches
of this shrub are an unmistakable sign of spring.

Forsythia's bright yellow blooms develop before the leaves of the shrub emerge.

Forsythia is named for William Forsyth,
royal head gardener and one of the founders
of Britain's Royal Horticultural Society.

In Chinese herbology, forsythia is respected for its power to clear away toxins, and it is used in some remedies for skin infections.

GARDENIA
MEANING: SECRET LOVE

Dark green, glossy foliage is a striking backdrop
to pale, scented flowers.

With their beautiful scent and stunning white flowers, gardenias are understandably popular. But they are very difficult to grow, since they're native to tropical areas.

Gardenias can grow to be 45 feet tall,
though few reach that size.

The gardenia blossom is used as a yellow dye.

Gardenias are classically used in corsages,
where they add their perfume to a special evening.
In France, they are used as boutonnieres
for men in evening dress.

GERANIUM
MEANING: TRUE FRIENDSHIP; FOLLY

These cheerful garden stalwarts boast vibrant
flowers held on tall stems above thick leaves.

The name geranium comes from
the Greek word *geranos*, meaning "crane,"
because the shape of the seed head is said
to resemble the long-necked bird.

British botanists brought geraniums
to England in the 17th century, and
Thomas Jefferson brought the first geraniums
to the U.S. in 1786.

Some geraniums have scented leaves, which can be used in cooking or dried and used in sachets.

Geraniums have many medical uses.
The roots contain tannins, which can be soothing
to people with stomach problems.

GLADIOLUS

MEANING: SINCERITY;
STRENGTH OF CHARACTER; INFATUATION

Tall spires display trumpet-shaped flowers
above sword-shaped leaves.

The gladiolus is named for the shape of its long, sharp leaves. The name is based on the Latin word *gladius*, meaning "sword." It is also sometimes known as the sword lily.

Botanists started breeding gladioli in the 1700s. Three centuries later, most gladioli in gardens and bouquets are hybrids, although you can still find wild species in the Mediterranean and Africa.

Gladioli are lasting as cut flowers,
displaying vibrantly for up to two weeks.
They are also easy to grow.

HEATHER

MEANING:

LAVENDER: ADMIRATION

WHITE: PROTECTION

An evergreen shrub with tiny leaves enlivens
moors with its purple flowers.

The name heather derives from a Scottish word, *haeddre*. In Scotland, where heather is the national flower, white heather is believed to bring good luck and is often included in bridal bouquets.

Heather flowers are tiny but each can produce
up to 30 seeds, making for very prolific plants.
The plants are also very hardy, with the toughest
bark of any shrub.

It is said that when heathers bloom abundantly
in the summer, a severe winter will follow.

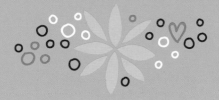

HONEYSUCKLE

MEANING: BONDS OF LOVE; GOOD LUCK FOR LOVERS

Climbing shrubs or vines are covered
with small, sweetly scented flowers popular
with birds and insects.

Hummingbirds love honeysuckle nectar.

Honeysuckle flowers are edible and have
a delightful, sweet taste, but the berries
are poisonous.

Planted by your front door, honeysuckles
are reputed to keep fevers and bad spirits out.
In some parts of Europe, it is believed that
honeysuckle blooming by your door will bring
a wedding within the year.

In traditional Chinese medicine, honeysuckle
is used to calm feelings of homesickness.

HYACINTH

MEANING: RASHNESS
BLUE: CONSTANCY
PURPLE: FORGIVE ME
PINK: PLAYFULNESS
WHITE: LOVELINESS

The hyacinth's fragrance announces
the plant even before the dense collection
of small, bell-shaped flowers that herald
the spring is in sight.

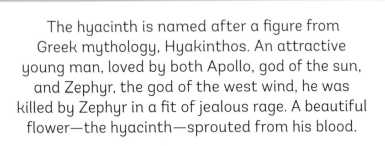

The hyacinth is named after a figure from Greek mythology, Hyakinthos. An attractive young man, loved by both Apollo, god of the sun, and Zephyr, the god of the west wind, he was killed by Zephyr in a fit of jealous rage. A beautiful flower—the hyacinth—sprouted from his blood.

In some cultures, the hyacinth is associated with rebirth. It is used as part of the Persian New Year celebration, Nowruz.

Hyacinths contain oxalic acid, which can irritate
the skin, so gardeners should wear gloves
while planting bulbs or cutting back
the plants after flowering.

IRIS

MEANING: HOPE, WISDOM, FAITH

Showy flowers in purple, white, or yellow rise
proudly on tall stems.

The fleur-de-lis, a stylized iris, has served as the symbol of France since the 12th century. Although the word *lis* in French means lily, French naturalists agree that it actually is an iris that is depicted in the fleur-de-lis.

In Greek myth, Iris is the messenger of the gods,
who traveled along the rainbow to bring
messages from the heavens to Earth.
She's a goddess of the sea and sky, responsible
for bringing water to the clouds to generate rain.

The rhizome, or root, of the iris can be dried—
for a minimum of five years—and ground to be
used in potpourri and perfumes. It's also found
in some spice blends, such as ras el hanout,
used in Moroccan dishes. The dried root
is known as orris root.

JONQUIL

MEANING: AFFECTION RETURNED

The modest appearance of these small, delicate flowers in yellow, cream, or white contrasts with their sweet scent and hardy nature.

In China,
jonquils are a symbol of good luck
for the New Year.

Jonquils were a favorite of
England's Queen Anne,
who planted them throughout
Kensington Palace Gardens.

Native to Portugal and Spain,
jonquils grow best in warmer climates.

LAVENDER
MEANING: DEVOTION, VIRTUE

Rising on spikes above narrow, scented leaves, lavender flowers can be violet or blue or even sometimes yellow.

The ancient Romans used lavender to perfume their baths. In fact, the name lavender derives from the Latin *lavare*, meaning "to wash."

Sachets of dried lavender tucked among your clothes will repel moths and other insects.

Lavender's essential oil has a balancing effect on the emotions, calming the mind and lifting the spirits. It can restore energy and vitality if you feel run down or exhausted. A tea made with lavender can help ease headache and stress.

As one 16th century writer noted,
lavender is "of especial use for all the griefs
and pains of the head and heart."

Lavender owes its memorable scent to around 180 different volatile ingredients. It's used in many perfumes to add a fruity essence. The best essential oil for perfumes comes from lavender grown in the south of France.

LILAC

MEANING:

PURPLE: FIRST LOVE

WHITE: JOY OF YOUTH

Lilac's fragrant purple, white, or pink flowers bloom in the spring on bushes that can grow as tall as trees.

A lilac planted outside your door may help
protect you from evil spirits, but some people believe
it's bad luck to bring lilac blooms into the house.

The botanical name of lilac is Syringa,
which comes from the Greek for "flute."
Lilac stems are naturally hollow and can be
used to make flutes or even the
stems for pipes.

If you cut lilac to bring indoors, bash the bottom of the woody stems with a hammer before plunging them into cool water. If they start to droop, recut the stems and soak them in a few inches of boiling water to revive them, then arrange them in the vase in deep, cool water.

LILY

MEANING:

ORANGE: HATRED
WHITE: PURITY
YELLOW: JOYFULNESS
DAY LILY: CHINESE SYMBOL FOR MOTHER
TIGER LILY: WEALTH, PRIDE

Large and fragrant flowers in white,
yellow, orange, pink, or purple return
every year, blooming in
the warmer months.

Lilies were potent symbols in ancient mythologies. They were associated with Ishtar, the Near Eastern goddess of creation and fertility. In Greek mythology, lilies were the sacred flower of Hera, the wife of Zeus and the protector of married women.

Lily bulbs are edible both fresh and dried.
The flowers are also edible and are said to have
general health benefits and to help with lung
conditions. Their oil is a marvelous skin conditioner.

Lilies grow easily in well-drained soil in temperate climates. Some striking examples grow as tall as six feet, but most are two or three feet tall.

LILY OF THE VALLEY

MEANING: SWEETNESS

Its delicate bell-shaped flowers rising on narrow
stems over broad leaves, lily of the valley has
a sweet scent that belies its poisonous nature.

The lily of the valley is associated with many superstitions. It's said to be bad luck to bring the flower indoors. In some places, there's a saying that "he who plants lily of the valley will die within the year."

Popular in wedding bouquets, lily of the valley
was the choice for Grace Kelly
when she married Prince Rainier of Monaco,
and for Catherine Middleton when she wed
Britain's Prince William in 2011.

All parts of the lily of the valley are poisonous, even in small amounts. It's essential to get immediate medical help if any amount is swallowed.

MAGNOLIA
MEANING: NOBILITY

Large, creamy-white, fragrant flowers grow
on evergreen shrubs and on magnificent trees
that can reach 80 feet tall.

The magnolia is an ancient plant, which appeared on Earth long before humankind. There are fossils of magnolias dating back at least 20 million years.

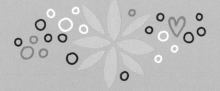

The magnolia is the emblem of the American South and is the state flower of both Mississippi and Louisiana.

The petals of magnolias are not true petals—
they're leaflike growths, known as tepals,
which are sturdier than petals.

MARIGOLD

MEANING: GRIEF, JEALOUSY

Easy to grow, these cheery blooms in orange
or yellow rising over narrow leaves are found
in gardens around the world.

Marigolds will attract ladybugs to your garden and also deter pests. They're popular as companion plants to tomatoes, eggplant, and chiles, but they shouldn't be planted near legumes.

Marigold flowers can be used as an inexpensive substitute for saffron or tarragon.

A marigold infusion is a delightful hair rinse,
and will give you shiny locks.

In Nepal, India, and Thailand,
marigold flowers are popular in decorations
for weddings and festivals.

NASTURTIUM

MEANING: CONQUEST, PATRIOTISM

Abundant, bright flowers in red, yellow, or orange
grow around rounded leaves with white spots
in their centers.

The name nasturtium derives from the
Latin for "nose-twister."

Nasturtium blossoms and leaves have a delicate spiciness that is tasty in salads—the hotter the sun while they're growing, the spicier they'll be. The blossoms are rich in vitamin C and lutein.

Nasturtiums are great "companion plants" in your garden, as they are natural pest deterrents. The seeds are large and sprout easily, making them ideal for a child's first flowerbed.

ORANGE BLOSSOM
MEANING: MARRIAGE AND FRUITFULNESS;
INNOCENCE AND PURITY

Clusters of the five-petaled white flowers are
a fragrant hint of the tasty fruit that follows.

In many cultures, women are adorned with orange blossoms or carry them in their wedding bouquets. Queen Victoria's orange-flower wedding bouquet started a craze for the flowers in England, though they were expensive and difficult to obtain.

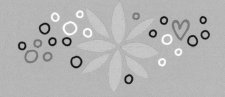

Orange blossoms have dual meanings.
They represent innocence and purity, thanks
to their pure white coloring. But they also
represent fruitfulness in marriage, because the
orange tree, unlike most other fruit trees, can be
in flower and in fruit at the same time.

A tea of orange blossoms can help fight anxiety and insomnia and is also an aid to digestion.

ORCHID

MEANING: LOVE AND BEAUTY

Exotic and alluring, orchid blooms are noted
for their strikingly delicate, symmetrical beauty
and their sweet scent.

There are as many as 25,000 species of orchids.
There are four times as many orchid species
as there are mammal species, and they are found
on every continent except Antarctica.

The vanilla plant is a member of the
orchid family.

Orchids get their name from the Greek word
orchis, meaning "testicle," after the shape of their
roots. In ancient Greece, it was thought eating
orchids could determine the sex of a baby:
If the father-to-be ate orchid root, it would be a
boy, but if the mother did so, it would be a girl.

Many people are passionate orchid collectors and some spend thousands of dollars acquiring rare plants. Orchids, however, are challenging to grow, and each species has subtly different needs.

PANSY

MEANING: LOYALTY; THINK OF ME

Colorful, cheery, three-petaled flowers,
sometimes resembling little faces with beards,
brighten any garden.

The name pansy comes from the French word *pensée*, meaning "thought."

The cultivated pansy we know today is very
different from its wild cousin, the viola.
Growers started crossbreeding pansies in
the 19th century to develop bolder flowers
and new color combinations.

Pansies are biennials, with a two-year life span.
They produce flowers and seeds only
in their second year, and then they die.

In King Arthur's time, the Knights of the Round Table would use pansies to tell the future. A knight would pluck a petal and examine the lines in it for signs.

Pansies have been used to cure heart conditions,
epilepsy, tumors, and skin problems.
A tea made from pansy flowers can help calm
a cough, and ointments made with pansies
can soothe irritated skin.

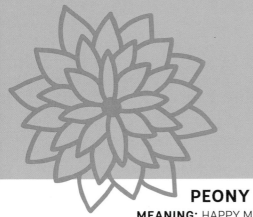

PEONY

MEANING: HAPPY MARRIAGE

Like a rose without thorns, lush colorful flowers
grow above bush-like greenery.

The peony is named for Paeon, a student of Asclepius, the Greek god of medicine. When Asclepius become jealous of his student's learning, Zeus protected Paeon by turning him into a flower.

The peony has many uses in Eastern medicine.
The root of the white peony is used to treat
stomach pains and as a tonic for women.

In feng shui, the pink peony is used
to encourage love and romance.

Ants are attracted
to peony buds because of their sweet nectar.
For many years gardeners believed that
the plant needed the ants to pollinate the bulbs,
but in fact, the ants disappear
once the bloom is open.

Peonies will last long in bloom in vases, and the petals won't spot indoors as they do outside. It's important to keep the stems long and bring the flowers in before they are fully open.

POPPY

MEANING: IMAGINATION
RED: PLEASURE
WHITE: CONSOLATION

Showy flowers boast paperlike petals around
dark centers in early summer.

Poppies have long been
a symbol of sleep, perhaps because one species,
Papaver somniferum, is the source of opium.
In *The Wizard of Oz*, Dorothy and her friends
wander through a poppy field and almost fall
into a permanent sleep.

The poppy is associated with
Remembrance Day, November 11,
honoring the soldiers who perished in World War I.
The WWI battlefields of Flanders and northern
France were covered with poppies, because the
flowers grow where the soil has been disturbed.

In some places, it is illegal to grow poppies. Yet they are beautiful perennial flowers that grow easily in sunny spots in the garden.

ROSE

MEANING:

DARK RED: MOURNING

PINK: PERFECT HAPPINESS

RED: I LOVE YOU!

WHITE: INNOCENCE

MIXED RED AND WHITE: SYMBOL OF ENGLAND

YELLOW: JEALOUSY

ROSEBUDS: INNOCENT HEART

Beautiful, often richly scented flowers are protected by the sharp thorns growing on their woody stems.

A bunch of roses was found in the tomb
of the Egyptian pharaoh Tutankhamun, and
Cleopatra reputedly had her pillows stuffed daily
with fresh rose petals.

All roses are edible, but the darker the flower,
the stronger the sweet flavor.
The white portion of the petals is a little bitter.

Rosehips, the fruit of the flower,
are very rich in vitamin C.
Harvest them before they're eaten by birds
and they can be used to make tea or jam.

The fragrance of roses can be captured
in rose oil, known as attar of roses, which is made
from crushed and steamed petals and is used
in perfume. Rose water adds a delicate rose
scent to foods.

The rose has been the symbol
of England since the 15th century.

What's in a name? that which we call a rose
By any other name would smell as sweet...

—ROMEO AND JULIET, ACT II, SCENE II

SNOWDROP

MEANING: PURITY, HOPE

The sight of these little bell-like, white flowers
brings hope that winter is ending.

The scientific name for the snowdrop
is Galanthus, from the Greek meaning
"milky-white flower."

There's a German folktale recounting the time
when the earth was first being created;
the snowdrop was generous enough to share its
color with the snow, and as a result, it's the only
flower that is unharmed by a snowy blanket.

Snowdrops are poisonous if eaten.
Scientists are experimenting with snowdrops
because they've found that one of the substances
in it can slow Alzheimer's disease.

SWEET PEA
MEANING: FAREWELL; BLISSFUL PLEASURE
Leafy vines with sweetly scented pastel flowers
climb six feet above the ground.

It is said that sweet-pea seeds planted on Saint Patrick's Day, before sunrise, will have larger flowers.

The poet John Keats wrote a verse about the flowers in "I stood tip-toe upon a little hill":

Here are sweet peas, on tiptoe for a flight
With wings of gentle flush o'er delicate white
And taper fingers clutching at all things,
To bind them all about with tiny rings.

TULIP

MEANING: FAME
RED: DECLARATION OF LOVE
YELLOW: SUNSHINE

Striped and solid, in all colors including a purple so dark it's almost black, tulips rise on their tall stems in the spring.

Tulips are native to Spain, North Africa, Greece, Turkey, the Middle East, and even Siberia. They were first cultivated in Persia, around the 10th century, but today the Netherlands is the biggest grower and distributor of flowers and bulbs.

During Tulip Mania, from 1634 to 1637, tulips were so popular and in demand that the price rose astronomically. They were so expensive that bulbs were traded like currency.

Tulip stems grow upright but if you display them as cut flowers, the stems will bend and twist around each other.

VIOLET

MEANING: MODESTY, LOYALTY, DEVOTION

Small purple flowers bloom over little heart-shaped leaves.

The scent of violets is fleeting.
One of the components of the flower's fragrance
is ionone, which temporarily dulls the nerves
in your nose, so you can't smell the perfume
for a few moments.

The leaves and flowers of violets
are a fresh and colorful addition to salads.
The flowers are often candied
and are a popular old-fashioned sweet.

About the Designer

The sculpture design in this edition was created exclusively for ArtFolds by **Luciana Frigerio**. Based in Vermont, Luciana has been making photographs, objects, book sculptures, and artistic mischief for over 30 years. Her work has been exhibited in galleries and museums around the world. Luciana's artwork can be found at: www.lucianafrigerio.com, and her unique, customized book sculptures can be found in her shop on the online crafts market Etsy at: www.etsy.com/shop/LucianaFrigerio.

The ArtFolds Portfolio

Color Editions

These smaller ArtFolds editions use a range of colors printed on each page to make each sculpture a multi-colored work of art. Titles now or soon available include:

Edition 1: Heart
Edition 2: Mickey Mouse
Edition 3: Christmas Tree
Edition 4: MOM
Edition 5: Flower

Classic Editions

These larger ArtFolds editions include the full text of a classic book; when folded, book text appears along the edges, creating a piece of art that celebrates the dignity and beauty of a printed book. Titles now or soon available include:

Edition 1: LOVE
Edition 2: Snowflake
Edition 3: JOY
Edition 4: READ
Edition 5: Sun

To see the full range of ArtFolds editions, go to www.artfolds.com.